MW01054269

The Unlucky Donkey

Written by Dr. Amanda Ellis-O'Quinn

Illustrated by Teresa Wilkerson

To Brenley and Ella, who always needed a story.
To my parents, who taught me to live without limits.
To Wade, for being my rock and giving me Zeke.

The Unlucky Donkey

Written by Dr. Amanda Ellis-O'Quinn
Illustrated by Teresa Wilkerson
Book design by Tara Sizemore
Published February 2016
Little Creek Books
Imprint of Jan-Carol Publishing, Inc

Copyright © Dr. Amanda Ellis-O'Quinn
ISBN: 978-1-939289-84-1
Library of Congress Control Number: 2016932409

You may contact the publisher:
Jan-Carol Publishing, Inc
PO Box 701
Johnson City, TN 37605
publisher@jancarolpublishing.com
jancarolpublishing.com

Jan-Carol
Publishing, Inc
"every story needs a book"

Dearest Child of God,

As you read the story that God scribed on my heart, my prayer is that you realize God created everyone with an extraordinary purpose, just like *The Unlucky Donkey*. Please refuse to believe any labels or limits that have been placed on you and know that even through adversity God can use you! Yield to His perfect plan and refuse to live life with limits. See yourself as God sees you by looking at your reflection in His word!

Let your light shine bright,
Amanda

Acknowledgments

In memory of my Aunt Ruth, who made this book possible. May her legacy live on.

On a small farm, just outside of Jerusalem, a baby donkey was born. The farmer was saddened when he first saw the donkey. The baby donkey was born with a strange marking on its back—a sure sign of bad luck. The farmer's heart was sad because he knew he couldn't keep the unlucky donkey.

Feeling sorry for the poor animal, he decided to tie the baby donkey to a post on the road leading out of town. The farmer hoped that someone would find a use for this unlucky donkey.

Soon a shepherd boy, who was leading his flock to a nearby field heard the pitiful cries of the poor animal. The shepherd, named Luke, followed the cries and found the baby donkey. When Luke saw the donkey, he quickly realized why it had been deserted. The donkey had a strange marking on his back, which meant he was bad luck.

As Luke looked into the animal's soft brown eyes, he could not bear the thought of leaving him and decided he would take his chances. Luke got very lonely tending to his flock and often longed for a friend. As he stroked the animal's soft coat, he thought his new companion could also keep him warm on cold nights.

That night as Luke was cuddled up to the small donkey, he began counting the stars in the sky. As he gazed up at a sky that never seemed to end, he couldn't help but to think that everyone has a purpose, even an unlucky donkey. He decided that the donkey deserved a name.

As he watched the little donkey grow stronger in the passing days, he decided to call him Zeke. It meant "God strengthens," which seemed quite fitting. By day, Zeke used his strength to clear the path for the flock. By night, he provided warmth and comfort for Luke. They were the best of friends.

One day as Luke and Zeke were tending to their flock, they noticed a crowd in the valley below. Overwhelmed by curiosity, Luke and Zeke made their way to the valley to see what was happening. They were surprised to learn that the large crowd was gathering to hear a teacher speak.

Unable to pull himself from the teacher's voice, Luke listened as the teacher shared good news of an everlasting love that comes from a Father above. Luke knew deep inside that this love must come from the same person who filled the night's sky. As Luke followed the teacher's lead and began praying, he felt like a new person.

As he scurried back to his unattended flock, Luke was overwhelmed with emotion. That night when he laid his head down on Zeke, he began to pray. He asked God to show him how he could be of service to Him.

As Luke was sleeping, God spoke to him in a dream. He asked him to take Zeke back to the post where he had found him and leave him there. When Luke began to protest, God made it clear that sometimes serving Him means giving up the things we love the most.

When Luke woke, there was an ache in his heart. He knew that God had answered his prayer from the night before. With tears in his eyes, Luke led Zeke back to the post where he had found him years before. As he looked into those soft brown eyes for the last time, it looked like Zeke was smiling at him. Trusting in God's plan, he sadly walked away from Zeke.

The next day, he returned back to the post to see if Zeke was still there. To his surprise, Zeke was gone.

In the distance, he could hear faint chanting. As the chanting got louder, the words became clear: "Hosanna! Hosanna! Blessed is the one who comes in the name of the Lord!" As Luke got closer, he saw a crowd waving palm branches and spreading them over the road that led to Jerusalem.

Luke couldn't believe his eyes when he saw who was coming down the road. To his surprise, there was his beloved friend Zeke, with no other than the teacher, Jesus, riding on his back. As they passed by, Zeke seemed to give Luke the same smile he had given him the day before.

It seemed the unlucky donkey had served a purpose after all—a greater purpose than Luke could have ever imagined. It turns out Zeke's marking wasn't really unlucky.

> ## "For I know the plans I have for you, declares the Lord."
> ### Jeremiah 29:11

Five hundred years before, the prophet, Zechariah, foreshadowed this event saying, "Be full of joy, O people of Zion! Call out in a loud voice, O people of Jerusalem! See, your King is coming to you. He is fair and good and has the power to save. He is not proud and sits on a donkey, on the son of a female donkey." (Zechariah 9:9 NLV)

Family Discussion Guide

1. What was the marking on Zeke's back? What does the symbol stand for? Was it really unlucky?
2. Was Zeke stereotyped or labeled because of his marking? What is a stereotype? What are some stereotypes placed on people today?
3. Has there ever been a time when you felt "unlucky" or like you weren't good enough? Describe that experience.
4. Is there anyone who is truly "unlucky" or does God have a special purpose and plan for everyone?
5. What are some gifts or talents that you feel like God has given you? How could you use them for Him?
6. When someone makes us feel like we aren't good enough, what are some verses that we can recite?

Please help Zeke travel by having an adult take a picture of you with the book and then tagging us on our Facebook page, *The Unlucky Donkey*.

About the Author

Dr. Amanda Ellis-O'Quinn received a B.A. degree from Emory and Henry College in Public Policy and Community Service, completed a M.S. degree from Radford University in Community Counseling, and a Ph.D. from Old Dominion University in Community College Leadership. Amanda spent fourteen years in higher education administration at Southwest Virginia Community College. She recareered when God presented an opportunity for her to work full-time in ministry at Highlands Fellowship Church as the Central Director of Children's Ministry. In 2016, she joined the staff of the church where she grew up, Community Heights, as the Director of Family Outreach. Amanda also works part-time as a private practice therapist. She has published several academic articles and enjoys public speaking. She holds positions on several boards and non-profits in her hometown of Richlands, Virginia. She feels her greatest accomplishment is teaching her children, Brenley and Ella, to be fully-devoted followers of Christ and raising them with her amazing husband, Wade. Contact the author at theunluckydonkey@gmail.com or on the Facebook page, *The Unlucky Donkey*.

CPSIA information can be obtained
at www.ICGtesting.com
Printed in the USA
LVOW05s1014120417
530553LV00024B/509/P